A Goc Impression

The story of printing in Fakenham

Jim Baldwin

Mark Baldwin

Dedicated to all Fakenham Printers past and present.

Originated by Fakenham Photosetting Ltd.
Printed by The Lanceni Press Ltd.
Bound by Dickens Print Trade Finishers

A Product of Fakenham

Preface

I clearly remember my first day at work as an apprentice. I was put to work with an older apprentice who, like me, is still 'in the trade' and has remained a friend to this day. The press that I worked on was already nearly forty years old and the company itself was nearly a century old. The working methods in use were modified versions of those which had been used for most of that time. In these last few years some incredible changes have taken place in the printing industry and equipment can be out of date within months yet one still has a sense of pride when looking at a book which one has had a hand in producing.

The trades that make up the industry have also changed. When I began work I joined the Typographical Association, a trade union representing letterpress compositors and machine minders. It was one of nine unions in the industry at the time whereas today the Graphical, Paper & Media Union represents those who work in all the disciplines of printing.

Fakenham is a printing town as a result of a quirk of history, like Beccles and Bungay in Suffolk and, although there were other printers in the town, this history is dominated by the company generally known as Wymans, although it started life with a different name and ended in the same way. There is no getting away from the fact that Wymans WAS Fakenham and had a great deal of influence on the town. After all, entire families worked there and two or three generations of families often worked there (my grandmother was a compositor). Apart from providing employment there were all the local services brought in by the company, such as the local watchmaker having the responsibility for all the clocks in the works and another supplying the paraffin! All this added up to quite a sizeable slice of the local economy.

It must be remembered that nearly 600 people worked at the Wharfedale Works at one point and it was the favourite saying of local people that 'I must get home before the printing works comes out'. Before the advent of shift working, a mass of humanity would fill White Horse Street and the environs at the end of the working day.

A good starting point for writing this book was the archive of

Fakenham Local History Society. When the Fakenham Press was closed, the Society took away as much archive material as it could lay its hands on! They always knew that it would come in handy one day and it certainly did! I thank them for the use of it and of their photographic collection. Reg Frost was also a great help, having spent a lifetime at Wymans. Keith Howell has also been a great help, beavering away in the Norfolk Record Office and on his PC to find all those missing bits that I needed.

There are so many people who have contributed to Fakenham's printing heritage over the years. In this book only the main players are named because there have been so many worthy of a mention that it would be difficult to know where to stop. Many of Wyman's employees worked there for fifty years, two directors, a father and son, gave ninety years service and a works director had a career of nearly thirty years. This sort of thing we shall never see again. Nor will we see the sort of long-term friendships born from meeting on the first day at work and remaining for the rest of a working life.

I am glad that I was able to be part of that before it died out.

Jim Baldwin

It seemed inevitable that I would end up in the printing industry in the town. After all, some of my family had been involved in the industry at some point as had most of my childhood friend's families.

I served my time as a lithographer at The Lancaster Press and was able to enjoy the experience of letterpress printing in addition to this. After spending some time out of the trade, the opportunity arose for me to return to work with my former colleagues as a result of a company merger.

It is this company, the Lanceni Press Ltd., who I must thank for their assistance during the production of this book. Thanks also to the late Richard (Dick) Chapman, Chris Woodhouse and Horace Defew for their help.

Finally, the Lancaster Press section of this book is dedicated to Frederick Woodhouse who took me under his wing as an apprentice and assured me that there would *always be a place for letterpress in the printing industry!*

Mark Baldwin

Ink on Paper
Stewardsons and others

At the beginning of the 19th century, Fakenham was a small market town with a splendid Church and a new Rectory to go with it. It also had two fine Coaching Inns but the Market Cross had been pulled down because it was unsafe. An almost new Independent Chapel was open as was a Methodist place of worship, but the Quaker meeting house had closed because it was in poor repair. A watermill was operating together with at least two windmills. But the question is - was Chadley Stewardson there?

Chadley Stewardson is thought to have been the first printer in Fakenham. If one can rely on the old saying of 'new house, new baby', Chadley Stewardson probably arrived in Fakenham around 1803 because his wife Abagail gave birth to their son Edward the following year. Their next son, George Nathaniel, was born in 1814. Chadley was certainly operating as a printer in 1819 when he had equipment capable of producing posters, broadsheets and pamphlets.

His rented premises were in Upper Market and the census of 1841 tells us that his sons George and Christopher were both apprentice printers with him. Within ten years George was running the business, living at Upper Market with his Norwich-born wife Anne and his infant son and daughter as well as a servant and a nursemaid. He traded as G. N. Stewardson, printer and his print shop was known as the Albion Offices after the type of printing press being used.

Following the death of his landlord, Henry Chapman Sayer, in 1856, George Stewardson bought the property for himself. Then, in 1860, he got permission from the Parochial Church Council to extend his building over the passageway leading from Upper Market to the Parish Church. So it was probably the Stewardsons who installed the carved wooden surround to the entrance of this passage which is still in situ today.

Like many printers of the day, Stewardsons had their works on an upper floor of the building which had been reinforced to take the considerable weight of the machinery and type. It could not have been easy to get the consumables in and the printed work out, let alone getting the equipment in in the first place! In later years a press was installed in the basement but there is evidence to suggest that this was not used to any extent.

The Stewardsons were also stationers and booksellers and towards the end of the 19th century and into the next it was this side of the business which was at the forefront, although they also sold pianos at one time! In 1883 the business was known as Stewardson & Son, suggesting that the eldest and unmarried surviving son George Nock Stewardson was now a partner, having returned from whence he went when he was 18!

George Stewardson died in 1886 and the business passed to George Nock Stewardson. Still unmarried he lived in the property at Upper Market with his sisters Kate and Mabel who were also described as printers and stationers. From around that time the business became known as Stewardson & Co. suggesting that all three were partners in the business. Sadly, George Nock Stewardson died at the early age of 45 in 1897 and on the 14th of July that year the reading of his will confirmed that he had left everything to his sisters, Mabel having married and moved to Essex by then.

In 1908 a directory of Fakenham carried an advertisement from Henry Stewardson, who had a shop in Norwich Street selling such things as gentlemen's shoes. If there was a family relationship it is not clear.

Another name crops up in connection with printing in the early 1800s and that is Platten. Chadley Stewardson had printed a number of flyers for a customer who was poking fun at a fellow townsman. The replies to this carried the printer's imprint of Platten. Quite who Robert Platten was is not clear. He is listed as a printer in Pigott's Directory of 1825 but he had gone by the time the 1839 edition was published.

A printer, by the name of Lunn, also operated in Fakenham during the 19th century but the only example of his work is a poster found on the basement wall of a shop in Norwich Street. It is interesting to note that this shop belonged to T. J. and later F. W. Miller, two people we shall hear about later.

It may be coincidence that an elderly spinster from London by the name of Lunn was living in the town in the latter part of the 1800s. Was this perhaps Lunn's sister? On the other hand a Lincoln-born man by the name of Earnest Lunn was an apprentice printer in Norwich in 1891. Could he have moved to Fakenham? He was, after all, the only person with that surname and trade in Norfolk at that time.

The Man From Wells
Thomas John Miller & Son

Thomas John Miller is credited with being the founder of one of the largest book printers in the country and certainly the largest employer Fakenham ever had, although it was his son Thomas John Miller Jr. who was the prime mover.

Miller Sr. was born in Wells-next-the-Sea in 1821, the youngest child of a baker by the name of Edmund Miller and his wife Ellen who came from Houghton (St Giles). By 1841 he was an apprentice printer lodging in Wells High Street with a baker by the name of George Morehouse. Why Thomas Miller was lodging with a baker in his own home town and learning the printing trade is not clear but it is quite possible that George Morehouse was also a printer although Pigott's Directory of that time does not list any printers in that town. On the other hand, the Miller family seems to have gone from Wells by this time, so the young Thomas may have been given board and lodgings by the Morehouses because they were friends of the Miller family.

We do know that, within the following five years, Thomas Miller had moved to Lower Market in Fakenham, where he was in business as a grocer and printer. During that time he had met and married Magdelene Coleman who was nine years his junior and had been born in Wickham Market in Suffolk. As a matter of interest Magdalene's name is sometimes recorded as Agnes and in the Fakenham Burial Register she is listed as Alice!

The shop in Lower Market seems to have been a busy one. Living there with the Miller family was Thomas' brother-in-law John who was an apprentice grocer together with Flitcham-born William Young who was also an apprentice grocer. Sophia Wilby from North Elmham was a *3*

Grocer's assistant and they were all looked after by Charlotte Wright from Hempton who was the house servant. Where did Thomas Miller get the wealth to allow him to run such a large household?

By 1854 Thomas Miller was a bookseller and was also publishing a newspaper called The Fakenham Advertiser.Four years later he purchased property in Norwich Street from Thomas Goggs and he branched out into selling china and glassware. This became Miller's Bazaar and was situated on the north side of the street towards its eastern end. It was this business which was later taken over by second son W. O. Miller when his father had reached the age of 60. Thomas Miller purchased some adjoining property to his shop from local veterinary surgeon George Baldwin in 1869 and within a couple of years he had built a new shop on it, giving his original property a new front to match. This original shop was later to be occupied by F. W. Miller, Thomas' grandson.

Thomas John Miller Jr. was born in Fakenham on 22nd October 1846 and seems to have inherited his father's printing skills which he put to good use when he was only sixteen years of age in 1862. He set himself up in business as a printer in his father's hometown of Wells-next-the-Sea. Wells was a very busy town, it had a thriving port and formed part of the huge Holkham Estate and so there seems to have been plenty of work for a printer. So much so, we are told, that Thomas Miller Jr. found he needed to expand his business. For some reason he could find no suitable premises in Wells and so, on his eighteenth birthday in October 1864, he returned to Fakenham. The local story is that he then set up his own business in the town, but it seems more likely that he took over his father's printing operation.

Two years later, in July 1866, Thomas Miller Sr. purchased property almost on the opposite side of Norwich Street to his shop. It comprised of the Sun Inn with various other buildings around it. By 1868 he had built a three storey building by the side of the Inn, described as a Printing Office, selling his interest in the Sun to Elizabeth Ann Brereton the same year. This Printing Office was then rented to Thomas Miller Jr. who traded as T. J. Miller Jr., employing a man and two boys. Although being only 22 years of age at the time, he must have had the backing of his

father.

This photograph of Norwich Street, taken about 1902, shows Miller's 'Printing Offices' just beyond the handcart.

As they are today: the former homes of Stewardsons, Miller's Printing Office and the Lancaster Press. *(Mark Baldwin)*

A postcard showing the local Hunt in the Market Place was produced by Stewardson & Co. for publicity. The picture may date back to the 1890s but the postcard is of a later date.

For some years Miller, Son & Co. Ltd. organised an annual *Wayzgoose* to Gt. Yarmouth for their workers, some of whom are seen here waiting for their train on the GER station. *(A. Gill)*

Local legend has it that 'Thomas Miller' walked or ran from Wells to Fakenham every day to work.

If this is true then it must have been Thomas Sr. because, by the time Thomas Jr. was going in the opposite direction, he was living only 10 minutes from the railway station!!

A special offer from a new newspaper!

The Pratt Bros. Lancaster Seed Works was situated in this building in Upper Market. The shop front was added some years later. *(Mark Baldwin)*

T. J. Miller Jr. Steam Printer seems to have been very successful, taking over the ownership of the Printing Office from his father in December 1877. Eventually he installed what is probably the most famous printing press of all time, the Wharfedale, which Miller Jr. adopted as the name for his printing works. This name was to last for one hundred years.

In addition to being a printer, Thomas Miller Jr. also had a considerable interest in photography and February 1887 he set up 'The Modern Studio' on the top floor of his works, boasting that it was open daily Rain or Shine. The conversion work was one of a multitude of jobs undertaken for Miller Jr. by builder Issac Fisher of Hempton who charged £10/3/- for the job, plus a few modifications from time to time. It is interesting to note that probably the last pictures taken by Miller Jr. were of the 1908 fire which destroyed a neighbouring shop in Norwich Street owned by Joseph Baker. Diversification seems to have been the watchword of the Miller family because a 'Refreshment Room' was also being run from this building during the mid 1870s!

The Wharfedale Works expanded to the rear of its Norwich Street frontage, but space was limited due to an accommodation road running behind it to serve all the other properties in the street. Land on the south side of this road was acquired and, in 1880, there is an indication that a local builder by the name of Needs constructed a new 'Machine Room' for the company. This was connected to the Norwich Street premises by a covered walkway over the accommodation road, linking the upper floors of the two buildings. Additional Wharfedale presses were then installed. It was this new building which was later destroyed by fire.

The following year an Otto Silent Gas Engine was installed at the works, Thomas Miller Jr. having seen it at an exhibition.

By 1881, Thomas John Miller Jr. was married to Sarah who came from Thursford and the couple had four children, Thomas Jarvis, Fred, Ellen and Ernest. The family were later to move to Wensum House in Hempton which subsequently became the headquarters of the Agricultural Worker's Union formed by Sir George Edwards.

Meanwhile, in 1861, Thomas Miller Sr. had bought the former Fakenham Poor House on Fakenham Heath together with land there for the princely sum of £700. Over the following years he built other properties on the land and then sold these with some of the land which paid off his mortgage. He then took out another! He was also allotted some land as part of the Fakenham Heath enclosure in 1871 and on a piece of this he built the Iron Mission Hut from which Mission Lane gets its name. This was opened in 1885 and services were held there on Tuesdays and, later, Sunday afternoons. Although it had a small stained glass window in its north end - it had an earth floor! It is said that the Mission Hut was built because Miller's tennants used the mile walk into the town as an excuse for not going to church! but in truth it was probably for Thomas Millers Sr.'s own use.

The previous occupier of the old Poor House had been the Revd. Legge who had built an extension, which included a chapel, on the soutnern end of the building. Thomas Miller sold this to his nephew E. W. Southwood in June 1873 with the rather odd covenant that no widow should inherit it! At the end of the day Miller Sr. had died, when the property became vacant because of Southwood apparently moving on. It was then inherited by W. O. Miller and, later, by one of his twin sons O. T. Miller.

By the time of the 1881 census the senior Thomas Miller had retired and was sharing his house with his wife and mother-in-law! His shop in Norwich Street had been taken over by his son William Osborne Miller who was still a batchelor living at home. The assistant in the shop was master J. Coleman who was his cousin and who also lived with the Miller household on The Heath.

Books
Miller, Son & Company Ltd.

By the late 1880s, the Wharfedale Works, with its trade motto of Speed, Economy had reached the stage when it was probably too big to be run as a 'sole trader' business Thomas Miller Sr. was in his late sixties and one assumes that he had little influence on the running of the business. To put the company on a proper footing, Miller, Son & Co. Ltd. was formed in 1890. Thomas Miller Jr. at the head of the company with

Thomas Jarvis, who had just turned 21 years of age, as the son referred to. Part of 'The Company' were Thomas Miller Sr., W. O. Miller and later F. W. Miller plus the bank and several other shareholders.

The Wharfedale Works may have gained a new imprint on its work but otherwise the company progressed as before. One noteable event was the building of the large boilerhouse chimney by local builder Issac Fisher who finished his work in 1892. This chimney was to dominate the Fakenham skyline for nearly a century and Issac Fisher's company was to become today's Fisher & Sons. Two years later the Norwich Street Printing Office building was surrendered by Thomas Miller Jr.'s son Jarvis to Wm. B. Denton who had probably loaned the money to Jarvis for the purchase at some point. This may have been a way of raising capital to finance the purchase of further land nearby for the expansion of the works. The Printing Office building continued to form part of the Wharfedale Works for a few more years.

By the end of the 19th century industry in Britain was properly organised and regulated. The Truck Act put paid to the practice of paying workers in kind and ensured that they received money instead. There were some protective employment regulations and the beginnings of trade unionism, but not too much in the way of health and safety regulations!

Being a progressive company, Miller, Son & Co. Ltd. conducted their business to the standards of the day and seemed to have the respect and loyalty of their staff, many of whom were skilled Journeymen.

Having said this, there was a considerable variance in the wages being paid as the century turned. Setting aside the fact that some workers, both male and female, in the composing room were on piece work, and that there were labourers, apprentices and boys on the payroll, earnings could be anything between 5/- (five shillings = 25p) and nearly £2.00. No two workers received the same wages and this is probably partly accounted for by the payment of 'extras' for different types of work or machines manned. It is amusing to note that the two employees who worked in the office and the two overseers had their names written in the wages book in shorthand. Quite what the point of this was when everyone knew who they were can only be guessed at!

Just to prove that there is nothing new under the sun, at the end of the year certain people who were not company employees were given

tips or 'backhanders' for services rendered to the company. The benefi-
ciaries ranged from the local police inspector to bill posters and public
houses. All received a shilling (5p) or two, except that is, for Mrs Pawley
who got 19/6 (nearly £1.00) for whatever service she provided!

All those who worked at the Wharfedale Works had to be familar
with the Company Rule Book. One of the most interesting things published in it are the hours of work which started at 8.30 in the morning.
Today, this seems a rather late hour for a factory to start and, since the
day went on until 7.00 in the evening, it could not have been for day-
light saving reasons. Was the 8.30am start giving time for the boilers to
get going? or was it, like so many other things in those decades, tailored
to suit the railway timetables!?

The Company Rule Book explained to employees all about the factory whistle and the 'clocking in' system, all works time being regulated
by Bone's Drum Clock in Norwich Street (next door to F. W. Miller's
shop). It also explained the various fines (payable into the sick club) for
breaking the rules including those aimed at boys to discourage them
from talking, gossiping, standing around and whistling. No smoking,
alcohol or newspapers were allowed in the factory. Six national holidays
were recognised and no male employee was to take any holiday during
the last ten days of July, which was a traditionally busy time for printers.

All persons employed in the machine, engine and boiler rooms were
to wear white jackets and trousers which were to be clean every
Thursday. The firm supplied one suit and the employee had to supply
the other. Bearing in mind the very dirty nature of these jobs, the choice
of white overalls is quite amazing!

The conditions of employment at the Wharfedale Works were very
fair for their time and the workers seemed to accept them, Millers were
a good company to work for and there was no other alternative in the
town anyway. From 1888 until 1900, employees were able to pay into a
social fund with which the company organised an annual Wayzgoose.
This comprised of a daytrip by train to Gt Yarmouth where all were
given breakfast and then a mid-day dinner in a hotel with all the trim-
mings of speeches and entertainment by the management and senior
10 employees. The highly decorative programme cards for these events were

mostly designed by compositor J. Ingall and printed by machine minder A. Crow. They are wonderful examples of a printer's craft.

Works outings continued after the demise of the Wayzgoose, but these were organised by the workers and were never quite as grand. Indeed they carried on into the 1960s, more often than not going to Gt Yarmouth!

Neighbours

E. W. Southwood

Apart from Thomas Miller Jr., one of the other tenants in Thomas Miller Sr.'s new building by the Sun in Norwich Street was Edward William Southwood. Southwood was a nephew of Thomas Miller Sr., no doubt the son of one of Thomas' sisters. He was born in London in 1840 and by trade he was a printer, bookseller, stationer and publisher. Arriving in Fakenham around 1860, he lodged with his uncle first in Norwich Street and then on Fakenham Heath. He seems to have worked closely with his cousin Thomas Miller Jr. which was to be expected with printer and publisher cousins trading next door to one another although, by 1875, he had bought himself a couple of blocks of property at the western end of the street. Southwood was also an acomplished chess player and in 1878 he published Chess Gems, a weighty tome written by fellow Fakenham man John Augustus Miles and printed by T. J. Miller Jr. The book must have been popular because it was taken up for future reprints by London publishers Adams & Co.

Like his relations the Millers, Southwood had a thing about diversification because a newspaper advertisement of his in 1880 describes his Norwich Street business as Southwood's Universal Suppliers offering not only stationery but provisions and groceries as well!

Another of Southwood's projects was the publishing of a Fakenham Directory but this seems to have been taken over by F. Blackett, a stationer trading in Norwich Street, who first comes on to the scene in 1883, by which time Southwood had moved to a Market Place address. Perhaps Blackett had taken over Southwood's business.

In 1885, A. J. Wheeler was running a stationery shop in Norwich

Street and it was he who was now publishing the Fakenham Directory. It seems likely that this was Southwood's business under yet another new owner.

A directory of 1886 lists Southwood, by now trading from premises in the Market Place, as being the publisher of The Fakenham & Dereham Times, then in its seventh year, which is still in circulation today as The Dereham & Fakenham Times. The agent was F. Blackett, Norwich Street.

It is likely that the Wheeler or Blackett stationery business was the business taken over later by F. W. Miller, Thomas Miller Jr.'s second son, some time between 1892 and 1896.

A New Century
Wymans

Thomas Miller Sr. died in May 1908 having outlived his wife by three years. His will decreed that his son W. O. Miller should sell the remaining property on The Heath within three years and that the money raised should pay off any outstanding mortgage. The balance was to be split between himself and his brother. The sale took place within a year.

The family who, by this time, were quite influential in Fakenham were also quite a large family as can be seen from the guest list at the wedding of Nellie Miller, Thomas Jr.'s daughter, in 1903. As well as Mr & Mrs T. J. Miller Jr., Mr & Mrs T .J. Miller Sr. were there together with Mr & Mrs T. Jarvis Miller, Mr & Mrs Ernest Miller, Mrs & Mrs F. W. Miller, Mr & Mrs W. O. Miller and the Misses Irene, Enid and Ethel Miller.

Nellie had married Mr R. O. Goddard, the private secretary to Lord Hastings and on the way from her home at Wensum House, Hempton, to the Church 80 girls from the Wharfedale Works threw flowers in the path of the couple which shows the regard that the workers had for the Miller family

At the Annual General Meeting of the company in April 1907 Thomas Miller Jr. was the managing director of Miller, Son & Co. Ltd. and was joint third largest shareholder together with the bank. Jarvis Miller was also a shareholder/director together with F. N. Webb of Cambridge and

J. B. Ellis of St Ives, who was the second largest shareholder. The largest shareholder was Gt Yarmouth brewer Sir Edmund Lacon, but he was not a director. Some of the remaining Miller family also had shares, W. O. Miller had the fourth largest holding while Thomas Miller Sr. and, later F. W. Miller, held smaller numbers. A number of local people were among the 60 shareholders of the company including H. F. Andrews who was a former employee now working as the printer at Stewardson & Co. Miller, Son & Co. Ltd. were without doubt the largest employers in the area and one of the leading book producers in the country.

However, in spite of their best efforts, things began to go downhill and the Miller family and their business were in trouble.

Miller, Son & Co. Ltd. was put into the hands of the Official Receiver. At the same time the business was being courted by the well-known stationery company Wyman & Sons Ltd. who had recently moved their printing operation from London to Reading and during 1908 they began the process which was to end with them buying Miller, Son & Co. Ltd., running it as an independent company and retaining the company imprint with the addition of Wyman & Sons Ltd. in brackets. In August 1908 a new company with the name of Miller, Son & Co. Ltd. was set up to run the business with seven nominal shareholders and with Henry Burt and E. Mackintosh of Wyman & Sons Ltd. as the directors. In fact these two were often the only directors of the parent company. H. P. Wells was the works manager.

This was the end of the Miller family's involvement in the Wharfedale Works and must have been a particular blow to Thomas Miller Jr. who had run it for some forty-five years. He remained in Fakenham for another year although, almost overnight, Miller Jr. and his family ceased to be the high-profile family that they once were. Indeed there is only one mention of Thomas Miller Jr. in all the 52 editions of The Dereham & Fakenham Times for 1908! The following year, needing a job he went to become manager of Carlton Roberts Ltd., who traded in The Broadway in Chesham, Buckinghamshire as The Carlton Press. He bought himself a house in Bellingdon Road and retained the position of manager when the The Carlton Press came into the ownership of F. J. Wilson in 1912 although, within a few years, he had retired. *13*

It must have come as some relief to the workers when Wymans eventually took over the printing works in Fakenham and presumably saved their jobs, although how much they knew of the situation is not clear. It was certainly not reported in the local press!

Quite what caused Miller, Son & Co. Ltd. to flounder is not clear either. It was probably its need to modernise to keep up with the opposition of companies like Richard Clay at Bungay and Wm Clowes at Beccles, two other situations where a quirk of history saw large printers operating in small rural market towns

An indication that this might have been the case is in Thomas Miller Jr.'s request to his old friend John C. Garrood to build an automatic sheet feeder for his printing presses. Garrood was a brilliant engineer, in fact he was the first to use tubular forks on the bicycles he built which were his stock in trade. He began work on an automatic feeder in 1900 but found the project slow going. He needed to cut paper to size for testing so he had to buy a guillotine, then he needed a shed to put it in and, finally, after some three years, he went to patent his invention only to find that he had been beaten to it and automatic sheet feeders were already in production.

During World War I John C. Garrood was retained as consulting engineer to Miller, Son & Co. Ltd. although his good friend Tom had long since departed.

This was also time for another member of the family to give up trading in Fakenham. F. W. Miller had been trading as a Stationer next door to W. O. Miller in Norwich Street since the mid1890s. It seems likely that he began trading around 1890 when he became 21 because, within two years, he is listed as a photographer. He may well have taken over his father's photography business possibly trading from a small shop one block away to the west from the old Printing Office. By 1896 F .W. Miller was a stationer in his grandfather's old shop on the other side of the street although some photographs of Norwich Street around the turn of the 20th century show the little shop still being occupied by F. W. Miller selling antiques, what diversity!

F. W. Miller also dabbled in the estate business after being left a
parcel of inclosure land on Fakenham Heath in a local will of 1899. The

following year he bought two more parcels of the same inclosure, one from his uncle W. O. Miller.

Records indicate that the business became a limited company in 1900, perhaps a way of raising capital for the family. Indeed, the major shareholders were his father's solicitors!

But all was not well for this member of the Miller family either. At an Exraordinary Meeting of F. W. Miller in October 1907 the shareholders were told that the company could not meet its liabilities and that a liquidator was being appointed. Horace Priest was the shop manager and it was he and his brother Herbert who took over the stationery and bookselling business, continuing to publish theTown Directory into the 1960s although under their own name of H&H Priest.

W. O. Miller had purchased the Norwich Street property from his father in 1901, replacing the shop fronts soon after this, and then carried on until he himself sold it in 1920. He had also bought some cottages called 'Cherry Pightle' in Norwich Road where he died in 1927. Some years later, two members of the third generation were trading and in the 1930s Gilbert Miller was making a living as a poultry farmer while Osborne Theodore was an Optician. They were the twin sons of W. O. Miller, Gilbert dying in 1968 and Osborne just over two years later.

The Wharfedale Works was still by far the biggest employer in the area with a staff of around 200 in a town with a population of just over 2000 and there had been no redundancies with the takeover by Wyman & Sons Ltd. To be fair, a number of the tradesmen were 'Journeymen' but the bulk of the workforce were local, with two generations of some families working there. Many of the employees were female and worked in the Composing Room under the supervision of a tradesman compositor, in fact the last female compositor finally retired in the 1960s.

Other females worked as sheet feeders in the machine room or as operatives in the bindery where there was much 'handwork' to be done, something that still continues today although to nowhere near the same extent.

Hardly had Wymans got a foot in the door when disaster struck. Between 2.00am and breakfast time on Saturday 21st November 1914 a large part of the Wharfedale Works was destroyed by fire, doing £20,000 worth of damage.

It was J.W. Readwin of Bridge Street who first spotted the fire, alerting his brother, who was second in command of the local fire brigade. They found both floors of the old Wharfedale Works, which was now in the centre of the complex, well alight as was a six-month-old boiler house on its western end. The fire brigade turned out both its steamer and manual pump which was used there for the last time. Water for the steamer was drawn from the new reservoir at the fire station in Hall Staithe on the other side of town while the manual pump was supplied from the town pump in the market place as well as a bucket chain of volunteers.

At the height of the fire flames were reaching a height of fifty feet and the brigade had to work hard to dismantle the walkway between the burning building and the offices in Norwich Street lest the fire should spread across and engulf all of the street. The East Dereham brigade were put on alert and were just preparing to make the twelve mile journey to Fakenham when, at 6.00am, it seemed that things at the Wharfedale Works were coming under control and so they were stood down.

Daybreak was a time to take stock of the damage. The old building had been destroyed, the composing room on the first floor had burned and collapsed into the machine room below destroying a score of Wharfedale presses. There was damage to the new Boiler House and some damage to the rear of Elliot's grocer's shop which backed onto the works from Bridge Street. Also backing onto the works from Bridge Street was the Post Office and a great deal of effort was made during the night to prevent this from catching fire. By some miracle the Fakenham to Norwich telegraph line was not cut even though it passed through the area. Wyman's recently completed addition to the works to the south of the Wharfedale Works, known as the Warwick Works, remained untouched, as did the eastern extension of the Wharfedale Works which was still under construction.

Wymans worked quickly to restore some sort of order. The following morning quantities of type and paper were delivered and some heaters were installed in a room of the recently vacated British School in nearby Norwich Road. Other sheds and buildings were also hired, including part of The Lancaster Press, and, since the Warwick Works had its own boiler and engine room, work resumed on the Monday morning with those employees who were employed in the burned out building being

The Miller men as they were circa 1906. Thomas Sr. is in the centre with Thomas Jr. seated on his right and William on his left. The three men at the back are the sons of Thomas Jr. while the boys are grandsons.

Staff of the Wharfedale Works survey the wrecked presses after the fire of 1914. The building affected was the one on the right of the chimney in the inset picture.

The Gospel Hall in White Horse St. is revealed by demolition work. It is thought that, somewhere in this area, a chapel was built for John Wesley, the father of Methodism, when he visited Fakenham in 1781. Sampson Pratt's Lancaster Press operated out of buildings behind his house in the background.

Right: A. A. Applegate (on the left) and his staff on the steps of Gresham Hall in 1927. *(H. Defew)*

Wyman's Bindery in the 1920s. The monogrammed roof brackets have been re-used in the Miller's Walk shopping arcade.

redeployed elsewhere. It is ironic that, had it not been for the fact that thirty men had gone off to join the Army, which was then four months into the Great War, they would have been laid off.

The Dereham & Fakenham Times reported that Thomas Miller Jr. had received many messages from both local and 'London' people for which he issued a statement of thanks and, at the same time, respectfully pointing out that he no longer had any interest in the company.

Within two years it seems that the works was back in production- certainly, aerial photographs of Fakenham taken circa 1917 show the factory to be complete. Cottages on the west side of White Horse Street had been sacrificed to provide a new frontage to the works, giving Miller, Son & Co. Ltd. a new address.

It would seem that Wyman & Sons Ltd. could see little point in continuing to run Miller , Son & Co. Ltd. as a separate company since they owned it lock, stock and barrel! So, at an Extraordinary General Meeting of the Company in March 1920, it was resolved that a liqidator be appointed to wind it up. The factory was to become an integral part of the Wymans operation, although the old imprint was to linger for a few more years.

The fire and the new company provided the impetus for some modernisation and new machinery was brought in, geared to the mass production of books, although the 'jobbing' side still continued for many years. As far as the machine room was concerned, Needs the builder returned in 1926/27 to build three additional bays and money was invested into additional large 'perfector' presses which could print either 64 or 128 pages at a time. Gone were the Wharfedale presses, although other machines from the same manufacturer were used for specialist work. It is interesting to note that, with the addition of automatic feeders, pile deliveries and some later rebuilding, some of these Perfector presses were still in use in the 1970s, although the longevity record must go to a Miehle Centurette press which was installed in 1915 and finally went out to a museum in 1981!

Eventually the composing room received Monotype type casting machines and it follows that the enlarged bindery, for which more cottages were sacrificed, had to become more automated. The company *19* then treated itself to some new offices, Needs the builder demolishing some shops on the corner of Norwich Street and White Horse Street to build them. They came into use in 1931.

All this rebuilding and new equipment gave the Wharfedale Works the means of producing hardback books for London publishers by the thousand and the company was also in at the beginning of the Penguin paperback catalogue, producing 32 out of the first 100 titles in 1936. Richmal Crompton's 'William' books were first printed in Fakenham and continued to be produced there for some forty years as were Enid Blyton's 'Famous Five' and 'Secret Seven' titles. Wymans also brought with them a contract from the Great Western Railway, printing it in the far eastern corner of the country!

Thomas Miller Jr. died in 1929 and the Miller, Son & Co. Ltd. imprint was gradually dropped, cutting the last of the family's links with printing in Fakenham, which had spanned some 80 years. From then on books from the Wharfedale Works carried the imprint of Wyman & Sons Ltd., Fakenham & London, later to be changed to the famous London, Fakenham & Reading imprint.

Meanwhile, across the road...
The Lancaster Press

One of the little mysteries of Fakenham's history is why Sampson Pratt decided to publish a newspaper in Fakenham in 1905. The town was already well served by the Fakenham & Dereham Times and other newspapers published in Norwich and King's Lynn could be brought in by the railways in just over an hour. Nevertheless, he gave it a try.

Sampson Johnathan Markham Pratt was born in North Elmham in 1857, a year later than his brother Robert. Their parents, Johnathan and Judith were part of the extensive Pratt family from Great Ryburgh and had moved to North Elmham where Johnathan was a farm baliff. By the 1881 census Robert was married with a family and lived in Oak Street, Fakenham, while Sampson was still living with his parents who, by this time, had retired to Hempton.

Both Sampson and Robert worked in the coach building trade at this time but before long they apparently decided on a change of direction and set up business as Pratt Bros., seedsmen and nursery men at the Lancaster Seed Establishment in Upper Market, almost opposite Stewardson's. Eventually Sampson married and moved into the living quarters there with his Fakenham-born wife Kate and by 1888 they had been joined by their son Donald!

By the time the census of 1891 had been taken Sampson's parents had moved, to live on Fakenham Heath, while Robert and his family had moved to Great Ryburgh ,where he became a farmer and head of the only family with the name of Pratt in a village which could once boast many! No doubt they had been living in tied accommodation when Robert was working for the coach builder in Fakenham.

By 1900 the business had moved to Whitehorse Street next to the old Independant Chapel, operating as The Lancaster Seed Company. Before long it seems that Robert left the business because, in 1910, it is listed as simply Sampson Pratt, Nurseryman.

Once on his own, Sampson Pratt branched out into printing and, given the name of his seed company, it was, perhaps, no surprise when the aformentioned newspaper went on sale as The Lancaster Press.

The first issue went on sale on Thursday 2nd March and contained a coupon which would entitle those who filled it in and returned it free accident insurance up to £100. A free 'situations wanted' advert could also be placed.

Unfortunately The Lancaster Press was not taken up by the public or, more to the point, advertisers. The twentieth edition in July of that year contained an editorial with a statement from 'The Captain' that the 'ship was out of commision'. It ended 'It is with great feelings of regret that we run the ship into harbour, with no intention, at least for a time, of taking another trip therein o'er the sea of liturature'. A footnote headed 'Practical' informed the public that 'the above remarks refer to the news-paper only' and that the printing business would be continuing for com-mercial printing.

With the financial loss no doubt absorbed by the seed business, the Lancaster Press carried on printing in the sheds behind the family home *21* and shop. After all, if the equipment purchased for the production of the newspaper could be made to pay for itself doing jobbing work there was no point in getting rid of it. This was a good move on the part of Sampson Pratt because the premises and equipment were later to be used extensively when the neighbour across the road, Wyman & Sons Ltd., suffered their serious fire in 1914 and arranged for some of their compositors to produce work at the Lancaster Press. One of these compositors was Alfred Ashley Applegate.

Following the First World War, Sampson Pratt found himself in poor health. He was still listed in Kelly's Directory as a Nurseryman , although it is assumed that he still had his small printing set up. By the early 1920s it seems that Sampson Pratt had given up his nursery and was looking to dispose of his printing business which, incidentally, was never advertised after the demise of the newspaper. This presented a golden opportunity for Alfred Applegate to branch out on his own. He could certainly do better than the 8/- (eight shillings) he was earning at Wyman's!

On 21st of January 1922 he formed The Lancaster Press Limited with Sampson Pratt. Each owned 60 shares, with Kate Pratt owning 5 shares, giving her and her husband nominal control. However, the partnership only lasted until 5th March 1924 when Alfred Applegate purchased Sampson and Kate Pratt's shares. Perhaps the ailing former seedsman was generous enough to give his friend a couple of years start before retiring altogether.

Sad to say, Sampson Pratt died in October of that year ,aged 67, with his wife outliving him by a further 6 years.

This purchase of shares from Sampson and Kate Pratt made A. A. Applegate the sole owner of the Company until the mid 1930s, when he sold some shares to two of his staff, and to his wife.

This new press needed a more substantial base than Sampson Pratt's sheds!, certainly if he only intended his involvement in the business to be short-lived. As soon as the Company was formed, overtures were made to the owners of the old Quaker Meeting House in Quaker Lane which, at that time, was being used as Bone's toffee factory. After a short while the application was rejected so, in July 1922, a board meeting resolved to rent Gresham Hall, the former Chapel in White Horse Street, for a period of 14 years with the option to buy.

The Independants had built this Chapel in the 1790s and when they built their new Chapel in Chapel Street (now Cattle Market Street) in 1819 the old building was taken over by The United Free Methodists who could boast members of the congregation who had built a Chapel, possibly close to this site, for John Wesley when he visited the town some 40 years earlier! The trustees eventually sold the building off into private hands and at one point it was tenanted by a Tinsmith by the name of Harrison ,who may well have been the same Harrison who built a house in Queens Road called Gresham House. This may be the origin of the name Gresham Hall for the old chapel.

Sampson Pratt had purchased Gresham Hall from the late Henry Read Culley's solicitors three months after the formation of the Lancaster Press Ltd. Following the board's decision to use this building, the tenant, Mr Richardson, was given notice to quit in October 1922 so that the Lancaster Press could move in.

So this was a case of the Lancaster Press Ltd. renting premises from one of its directors, something that Miller, Son & Co. Ltd. had done with their printing office in Norwich Street.

But this was not the first time Gresham Hall had been used by a printer ,since, in 1908, Miller, Son & Co. Ltd. had rented it from the then owner (George Strangleman, cattle dealer and former landlord of the Star Inn) for £15.00pa with an option of a seven-year lease.

Although the old Chapel was the obvious place to site the new company it did need a little modification to the building. This was paid for on a 50/50 basis by landlord and tenant. The equipment was moved in during early 1923 and the Lancaster Press Ltd. was gradually built up into a thriving business.

The option to purchase was taken up when Kate Pratt died in 1930. However, it was not the Company but A. A. Applegate who bought the building, which he then owned for the next eighteen years.

Another Newspaper
The Norfolk Chronicle

Both Thomas Miller Sr.'s and the Lancaster Press' attempts to provide Fakenham with a local newspaper did not go well. However, Southwood's Fakenham & Dereham Times survived and in 1957 it absorbed another Fakenham produced newspaper -The Norfolk Chronicle.

This paper had begun life in Norwich in 1761, eventually ending up in Holt where it was printed by Rounce & Wortley who later moved to North Walsham. By the 1930s it embraced a number of editions, one of which was The Fakenham Post and it is probably because of this that it was bought by Thomas Cook of Sennowe Hall near Guist. He was a descendant of the Thomas Cook who founded the famous travel company and by 1936 he had built a new (wooden) printing works in what is now Chronicle Lane in Fakenham. Although the factory has now gone, the lane still runs as a public footpath between the Norwich and Holt roads.

Thomas Cook installed four Linotype machines and a Cossor printing press getting the first three-edition paper off the press at Whitsun 1936. This had a circulation of 4,200 copies and by 1955 circulation of The Norfolk Chronicle had risen to 14,000 copies. Since it was now serious competition to The Dereham & Fakenham Times its publishers, The Norfolk News Company, bought it and incorporated it into their title. Most of the workers found jobs with Wyman & Sons Ltd.

The Presses Keep Rolling
The 1940s and 1950s

The 1930s were not the best of times for any business and Wymans were no exception. Although it comprised of a string of station bookstalls, a London newspaper distribution business and printing works in Reading and Fakenham the Company struggled. During this time it was unable to pay any dividends and in 1938 the Company had to restructure itself financially. However, production continued at Fakenham and the

Wharfedale Housing Society Ltd. was formed, buying land in Hayes Lane and the village of Pudding Norton where semi-detatched houses were built for the employees. Some cottages on the east side of White Horse Street were also acquired and demolished.A small warehouse was built on the site which was later used to house troops during World War II. Over the years that followed the remainder of the cottages on this side of White Horse Street were purchased either by the housing society or by the company for redevelopment.

War came again and this time it had far more effect on the Wharfedale Works; many of the men were called up for war service, indeed, a number were among those of the Norfolk Regiment who were captured by the Japanese and spent the war as prisoners in the far east. It is interesting to note that, when long-serving machine minder Bert Pearson retired, a list was found in one of his drawers containing the names of all those from the works who were away in the war and it seems that he attempted to write to them all. Someone else organised collections to pay for 'Parcels for the Troops'. To begin with these contained either cigarettes or tobacco but from the middle of 1940 money was sent instead. Each man serving in the forces would expect a parcel every couple of months or so but, significantly, after the fall of Singapore in early 1942, many names ceased to appear in the cash book. The last payments were made in the Autumn of 1945, with the exception of one in 1947 and another in 1948.

Producing books under wartime conditions was not easy but it did continue. To shortages of paper and staff were added a change in working hours, introduced as a result of the works having been built with glass 'north lights' in the roofs which were difficult to black out. The number of hours worked with lighting had to be reduced and, during the short days of December, much of Saturday was part of the working week. In addition to all this, the males remaining at work undertook fire-watching or Home Guard duties outside their working hours as well as 'Digging for Victory' so no one was really at their best. With all these difficulties to put up with, the employees of the Wharfedale Works still gave a thought to the wider war effort. During War Weapons Week in 1941 they raised £192/2/6 ,although the original target was £50.00 and the following year for Warship Week they put their hands in their pockets and collected £170/5/-. The Works also had a savings group of more than 120 members.

Fakenham was lucky to have escaped with very little war damage in spite of the fact that it was surrounded by at least eight aerodromes. When the works was cleared on its closure the air raids on the town were found chronicled in the back of one of the Stores Ledgers, somebody had given some thought to future historians!

Once the war was over ,things were very slow to get back to normal and, for some ten years, the methods and equipment remained those of the 1920s and 1930s. The only modernisation which did take place was the introduction of electrical power to the machinery in 1946. The Ruston Hornsby boiler, which had been installed in 1914 and the second which had gone on stream in 1926, were both made redundant and the boiler room was converted into an engineer's shop. The winter of 1947 did not help matters, with Fakenham having difficult communications with the outside world for some weeks because of heavy snow and men having to be deployed to clear snow from the roofs on several occasions. However, Britain slowly came out of the post-war period of austerity and towards the end of the 1950s a programme of introducing new methods and machinery and the rebuilding of some of the older printing presses had begun. Initially it was the composing room floor which was attended to when it was asphalted over in 1952. Even then, the composing room had not gone fully over to the 'point' system of measuring, something its smaller neighbour The Lancaster Press had done many years earlier!

One of the post war policies of Wyman & Sons Ltd. was to expand into the areas serviced by the Great Western Railway, with whom they had been long associated. They bought up a number of small stationers and printers, including Oscar Blackford Ltd. of Truro, to where much of the plant from two other printers was sent following their purchase and closure.

At this time, it became apparent to the directors of Wyman & Sons Ltd. that there was a possibility of a takeover bid being made by someone buying up shares from the smaller shareholders. For contractual

By the 1970s the Wharfedale Works dominated White Horse St.
Above: The east side in the early 1960s after the completion of the Eagle Star building. In the foreground is the warehouse built prior to the Second World War.

Below: The west side of the street showing the original front entrance to the works. The old Bindery in the background was originally a single storey building.

The other resident printer in the street was the Lancaster Press. The printer here proudly displays some of his work on the wall.
(Chris Woodhouse)

Wyman's Machine Minders and their assistants clear snow from the roof during the winter of 1947.

Right: New technology could not replace the platen for printing labels at the Lancaster Press. *(Lanceni Press)*

The Overseer and Machine Minder demonstrate the Timson Letterpress Rotary to the Directors. Eric Burt, centre, was the son of Henry Burt of Wyman & Sons Ltd. who saved the Wharfedale Works in 1908.

Below: Cox & Wyman's Litho Hall in Old Lane produced colour books for the world over.

reasons this would not have worked since the company buying the shares, Clarence Hatry & Associates, were involved in publishing which would have compromised Wyman's bookstall operations and would have seen the end of the Company. The board of Wyman & Sons Ltd. struck a deal with the Eagle Star Insurance Company to buy this person out. At the same time this brought in some Eagle Star people onto the board of Wyman & Sons Ltd. and with this extra backing the Company felt able to go ahead with a project to build a new composing room on the east side of White Horse Street, even though this would be separated from the machine room by a public highway! The plans had originally been drawn up in 1954 and work began on clearing away eight cottages and constructing this new building in 1957 which was used as the bindery on its completion. It was further extended in 1970 removing the remainder of the terraced cottages from White Horse Street.

The 1950s was also a time when more staff were being taken on and to house some of these the Wharfedale Housing Society Ltd. built some houses on land at Highfield Road in 1952, eventually calling it Caslon Close after a traditional typeface used at Fakenham. The building of these houses had been somewhat problematical because this was a time of an acute housing shortage in the area. All building was licensed by the government via the Walsingham Rural District Council who were keen to use their allocation to build houses to rehouse some of the 100 families living in Nissen Huts on two former aerodromes near Fakenham. In April 1951 the WRDC were allocated an extra 12 houses under the scheme for 'Dollar Export Workers' and these houses went to the Wharfedale Housing Society Ltd. Six more houses were built on this site in 1959 and in 1963 the first three pairs of houses were built on another estate off Wells Road which was to be named Clarendon Road after another popular typeface. Finance for this housing came by way of a 100% mortgage from the WRDC as did the finance for remainder of the houses on this site built over the following years. By 1969 the Wharfedale Housing Society could boast that it had built over 100 houses in Fakenham. In addition there were 19 under construction at Whitelands off Greenway Lane and six elsewhere, with plans for a final 17.

Still across the road...

With The Lancaster Press Ltd. now secure in its new home, it began to build up its potential as a serious jobbing printer. By October 1922 the Company was already producing many posters, local government work and small booklets.

Not only had the work been upgraded but so had the machinery. This included a Wharfedale Press and two treadle-operated platens, and by December 1926 another second-hand machine had been purchased for the sum of £80, a lot of money in those days.

Much stayed unchanged for the next couple of years until the company had become so satisfied with its progress that it was decided extra staff could be taken on. Two additional men were then taken on and in due course they were offered shares when the company began to feel the effects of the depression in the 1930s. The two new employees quickly accepted the offer and in doing so became directors of the company.

It seems that there was no stopping the press through the latter part of the 1930s as plenty of work was coming in. The two new employees received more shares in the company in due course with some of them being transferred from A. A. Applegate.

As war broke out in 1939 the Lancaster Press' financial situation was considered to be very satisfactory indeed. However, by the following year, with the rising price of materials and the war becoming more wide-spread, the balance sheets at the end of 1940 showed a big decrease in profits. Inevitably, by1941, members of staff were being called up for the services. This included the two employees who were allowed to remain share holders in their absence.

With the shortage of staff and the reasonable figures for the year so far, it was decided that the company should continue to trade and a young boy and girl were taken on to help out. The new recruits proved to be a great help. However, towards the end of the war it had become very difficult to carry on and with the directors away it was impossible to chair any meetings to come to a decision on the future of the company.

By March 1947 both directors had safely returned from the services and resumed their roles at the firm and to their relief, after a series of meetings, the balance sheet for the previous year was considered satisfactory enough for the business to continue. It was recommended by the directors that, due to the rising cost of living and a good financial year, employees wages were to be increased to £5/10 and A. A. Applegate's to £4/10 per week.

With the wage increase it was also suggested that the working hours should be reviewed. These were then changed to accommodate a 9.00am start and a 5.00pm finish.

These changes however did not bring the hoped for stability and in June 1948 Frederick Jude, one of the employee shareholders, called a meeting to announce his resignation, as he had accepted another job across the road at Wyman & Sons Ltd. (he was eventually to become works director). This was received with regret but his shares were not issued to other employees, as just a few months earlier problems had been discovered in the balance sheets.

This in turn led to A. A. Applegate deciding to put The Lancaster Press Ltd. up for sale in July 1948.

It has never been discovered quite how the balance sheet discrepancies occurred , but it would possibly seem that something was amiss due to the firm's poor performance during the latter part of the war and its sudden turn around. With this in mind and the fact that A. A. Applegate was at retirement age, it was inevitable that big changes were about to occur.

The sale of The Lancaster Press Ltd. was a very quick operation indeed. In fact it would have a new owner just three months later when, in October 1948, Mr Robert Andrews paid £1700 for the business. At that time Robert Andrews was running the printing operation that his father had taken over from Stewardsons earlier in the century. On acquiring The Lancaster Press Ltd. this business was closed down.

Robert Andrews acquired 98 shares from A. A. Applegate and 22 from the remaining employee shareholder. A further 5 shares were transferred from Mrs Applegate to Mrs Andrews, the wife of Robert.

At one of the first board meetings chaired by Robert Andrews, the leasehold of the premises, No 1 White Horse Street (Gresham Hall), was discussed. It was declared that A. A. Applegate had granted the company *31* first refusal for the purchase of the leasehold of the premises, for £600 in the event of A. A. Applegate wishing to sell it.

That year the remaining employee director decided to leave to take up an offer given to him by Wyman & Sons Ltd. and in doing so he sold his remaining shares and moved across the road, where he would remain for the rest of his working life.

In 1955 a former wooltrade worker by the name of Richard Chapman, took an interest in The Lancaster Press Ltd. when it was discovered that during Robert Andrews' time as major shareholder and director of the company, there were further problems with the accounts. The problem was eventually traced but it had put the firm in such bad financial shape that after several meetings with all the shareholders, Robert Andrews was advised to sell some of his shares.

In September 1955, Robert Andrews stood down as managing director with Richard Chapman receiving his shares, becoming the major shareholder.

One of Richard Chapman's first actions was to finance the upgrading of the company's machinery. This was mainly because the Wharfedale Press, which had been purchased from Scotland Yard many years earlier, was becoming inadequate. With this a new Thompson British automatic platen was bought to work alongside the Thompson the firm already had. (Incidentally both Thompsons are still in use in Fakenham at the time of writing, with one at Taylor Printing and the other still owned by The Lanceni Press). Another purchase was also made in the shape of a folding machine which, with the increasing work load, was an essential piece of machinery.

Robert Andrews and his wife sold their shares in the company and left the area and the trade in 1957. Things had settled down for The Lancaster Press Ltd. and minds were concentrated on the increasing workload.

With nearby RAF Sculthorpe now becoming home to many American servicemen and women, The Lancaster Press Ltd. found themselves in a very satisfactory position indeed as they were contracted to print a monthly newsletter entitled The Sculthorpe Scanner, a paper which found itself being read by a least 10,000 Americans all over Norfolk.

32   As well as the paper, the company produced tickets and posters for

dances and other events on the Base (as it was known locally) along with racecards for the Fakenham Racecourse and much local jobbing work. It is little wonder that an engineer was hired from The Eastern Daily Press to come out and service the Linotype machine on a regular basis!

The routine continued for the next few years, apart from extra staff being taken on. However,it was becoming difficult to work in the cramped conditions of the White Horse Street premises so the search began for larger premises.

The answer was found in the shape of an old garage in Holt Road and in 1965 The Lancaster Press Ltd. bought the building and moved in. The moving of the machinery was in itself an event with members of staff loading presses on to flatbed trolleys which were pulled by hand up to the Holt Road site!

Modern Times
Cox & Wyman

John Menzies, distributors of newspapers in Scotland, were looking to expand into England and, to them, Wyman & Sons Ltd. seemed the obvious choice of company to buy. They made the Wyman's board an offer that they could not refuse and gave them the option of buying back the printing side of the business. The deal was struck in 1959 and a new company, taking the ancient name of Cox & Wyman Ltd., was formed to run the factories in Fakenham, Reading and Truro with a sales office in London. There were many familiar faces from Wymans on the new board of directors.

This is, perhaps, an appropriate juncture to look at the way goods were brought into and sent out of the Wharfedale Works, Fakenham being way off any major transport route. In the early days the railway was the lifeline for the company but in 1940 Wymans switched to road transport, considerably reducing the traffic revenue of the former GER station. No doubt flexibility was needed in the adverse conditions of war. After the war there was a continued use of road transport with a local haulier getting most of the business. When Cox & Wyman Ltd. took over, this haulier was given the contract to supply services using vehicles with the Cox & Wyman logo. The company also had its own van for small load work.

It also purchased a fork lift truck to move the increasing amount of palletised work around the factory and back and forth across White Horse Street. This caused problems when the Highways Department wished to turn this street into a one-way road, it ended up continuing as a two-way road but with no entry at the north end. This gave the fork lift truck continued freedom to move up and down White Horse Street instead of having to do a round trip through the town for a return journey. Now that would have been fun on a market day!

For a time in 1958, waste paper was stored in a row of 107-year-old cottages in Old Lane before they were demolished by the local council at the tail end of their slum clearance scheme. No doubt that today these houses would have been renovated and a bit of Fakenham's history retained!

Cox & Wyman Ltd. faced the challenge of a nine-week national printer's strike as soon as they had taken the company over. Reluctant pickets sat outside the factory gate during one of the hottest summers for years while inside managers and apprentices undertook what limited production they could. The rest of the workforce went blackcurrant picking and returned to work fit and tanned!

Nevertheless, Cox & Wyman Ltd. lasted ten years as an independent company, continuing with modernisation and the introduction of new plant, demolishing the last cottages in White Horse Street in the process. A Timson Rotary reel-fed press was installed and was often called upon to work treble shifts to keep up with the workload. A sheet-fed DPE Rotary Press was also installed and new, custom built, binding lines were put in to finish the work that these presses produced. Both used flexible plastic plates produced on new equipment which was installed in the composing room foundry.

By 1968 the production of paperback books had been concentrated at Reading, who took the Timson Press, while all hardback book production was moved to Fakenham which by now was boasting nearly 600 employees! There is no doubt that these workers had seen some remarkable

Part of the Wyman's Machine Room in 1926 showing some Miehle Perfector presses (and their unguarded belts!). Some could print 128 pages of a book on one sheet.

During the 1950s and 60s some of these machines were rebuilt to give a few more years service.

The last letterpress printing machine, a Miehle Centurette, leaves Fakenham for the Rural Life Museum at Gressenhall in January 1981.
This particular machine was installed in 1915.
(Eastern Daily Press)

During 1968, the remaining cottages on the corner of White Horse Street and Old Lane were demolished to build a loading bay. It was this building which flew the Cox & Wyman flag on the company's last day of existence.

A Compositor working at his *Frame* correcting a line of type in his *Stick* using *Sorts* from a *Case*.

Below: Typesetting gradually gave way to Filmsetting. In the days before microchips the mechanics of the system were basically those as used for hot metal setting!

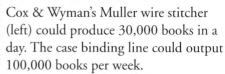

Cox & Wyman's Muller wire stitcher (left) could produce 30,000 books in a day. The case binding line could output 100,000 books per week.

This often included.............

......Monty Python books. Some of the bindery workers are seen here with the madcap entertainers. The reader is left to decide who is who!

changes during the preceeding decade. However, the production methods were predominantly those of the previous century, i.e. letterpress, although there had been a small experiment with litho printing.

All these changes were to be short-lived because, just as the rationalisation had begun to settle down a holding company, Thomas Tilling Ltd., made a bid for Cox & Wyman Ltd. in 1969, a bid which the board were happy to accept. The Thomas Tilling Group owned many companies including Heinemann the publishers and a third of Pan Books. But more importantly they owned Crawley lithographic colour printers Bookprint, who had grown out of the old Heinemann Windmill Press. This company was closed down and their operation moved to Fakenham in 1970 together with their sister company Bookprint International who specialised in organising the production of children's colour books in many languages. Although this latter company worked mostly out of the London Sales Office.

Space was found in the old Wharfedale Works for the initial delivery of Litho presses and work began on a brand new Litho Hall on land to the south of Old Lane. This was built by Fisher & Sons (Fakenham) and when it was opened in 1970 its 30,000 square feet made it the largest purpose built building of its type in Europe. Bookprint's colour litho presses were then moved in together with all the supporting pre-press departments which included the embryo filmsetting department.

Over the following years a new binding department was built beside this new building although the method of construction was nowhere as grand!

To service these litho presses with the necessary film for platemaking, Cox & Wyman Ltd., together with a company called Colour Workshop Ltd. formed Wensum Graphics Ltd. Initially housed in Sampson Pratt's old shop in White Horse Street they eventually moved to the former Congregational Chapel on the corner of Norwich Road and Ratcliffe Road which led to Old Lane where the new works was situated. They continued to supply Cox & Wyman Ltd. for the next five years.

With this influx of workers from outside the town came the problem of housing those who were not buying their own property. Some of the Wharfedale Housing Society's stock were being sold to the worker/ *37* tenants and there were no plans to build more. Cox & Wyman requested some 'Key Worker' houses from the WRDC and were allocated ten at Green Lane Estate, Pudding Norton in 1970. A further ten were refused. However, by the end of the following year the company advised that their requirement was now only two houses, changing their mind a year later when they wanted five and then seven! Some of the council houses on the emerging St Peters estate were allocated to retired Cox & Wyman employees.

The printers at Fakenham were now producing books the like of which their ancestors would never have imagined. 'Coffee Table' books became a speciality with many thousands of titles leaving the Fakenham works each week. Included among these were many reprints of Monty Python books together with countless numbers of HM The Queen's Silver Jubilee books and the definitive book on the Royal Wedding of HRH The Prince of Wales. Alongside these the works turned out large quantities of academic books and comic annuals, requiring the re-intro-duction of a Perfect Binding (paperback) line in the bindery. This was not for the 'Pan Books' type of paperback but for softback editions of mostly non-fiction type books of classics.

Unlike today, in past years printers would hold large stocks of paper in store which, by the 1960s and 70s, was held mostly on behalf of pub-lishers. Cox & Wyman Ltd. were no exception and as production increased so did the pressure on warehouse accommodation, so the company were obliged to look for places to rent until the new litho hall and its attendant buildings were available.

Cecil Wainwright's former piano warehouse was the most conven-ient. Situated at the end of what was once Wakefield's Yard off Bridge Street it backed on to the letterpress machine room. Whilst on the other side of town in Oak Street the Star Barn was rented. This former home of the Salvation Army became the company Social Club in 1972 when the need for paper storage became less acute. The following year the club raised more than a few eyebrows in the town when they held a strip show there! The Fakenham Press Social Club was renamed the Press Club after the closure of the printing works.

Serious national events took a hand in the future of Cox & Wyman

Ltd.when, at the beginning of 1974, a power crisis brought about by industrial unrest caused the works to be put on short-time working. The following year demand for letterpress printed books began to wane and the works was again put on short-time working in an effort to save jobs. However, by the end of 1976 it had become apparent that few publishers were considering letterpress books and the department was slimmed down and 40 redundancies announced. At the same time the bindery had completed its move into the new building by the Litho Hall so that the letterpress department could be moved into the Eagle Star building,leaving the old Wharfedale Works empty after nearly a century of use.

The 1970s may have been a time of dramatic events for the company, nevertheless there were times when it was felt fitting to celebrate. In 1971 the Wharfedale Works opened its doors to the public one Saturday in what turned out to be a very good PR exercise. Then, in 1976, the printing industry celebrated the 500 years since William Caxton first set up a press in the country. Cox & Wyman Ltd. at Fakenham organised a display in the local library and a special service at the Parish Church as well as opening the works to the public once gain. The following year Cox & Wyman Ltd. celebrated 200 years in business, producing a book entitled A Company History.

Old Names and New Names
Other Printers

With Cox & Wyman Ltd. dominating the printing scene in Fakenham it is easy to overlook the smaller businesses operating in the same trade. Stewardsons, by the turn of the 19th century, were trading as booksellers and stationers. From 1930 until 1937 their printing was being undertaken by Henry Frost Andrews whose business address was c/o Stewardsons. H. F. Andrews had come to Fakenham from Cambridgeshire to work as a reader for Miller, Son & Co. Ltd. Indeed, he had some shares in the company until it went into receivership. He left them in October 1903 to become printer at Stewardson & Co, perhaps taking the pressure off Kate Stewardson who could well have been running the *39* business single handed for the six years following the death of her brother. It would seem that, in 1930, H. F. Andrews took over the company's printing interests since this is when his imprint replaces Stewardson's although any work gained through the shop would still carry the old one.

His son, Henry Robert Andrews, took over after World War II but the business finally faded out when he purchased all the shares in The Lancaster Press Ltd. in 1948, taking his customers and goodwill with him. He also took the Parish Magazine which he had won over from Miller, Son & Co. Ltd. after he had joined Stewardsons. This publication began life as The Parish Magazine in 1885, later becoming The Church Magazine. It later lost its title altogether before reverting to The Parish Magazine. It is currently called The Fakenham Beacon.

Stewardson's book and stationery shop still continued in business and in 1965 made a planning application to replace the shop sign which was refused even though the original had been in place for as far back as anyone could remember! They still advertised themselves as printers but the work was 'farmed out', probably to the Lancaster Press!

Having been bought by W. J . Aldiss Ltd., Stewardsons were eventually to become the stationery and card section of Aldiss' department store next door, finally being phased out in 2000. The Lancaster Press had by 1965, moved to larger, more convenient premises in Holt Road where they took on new equipment in the form of offset lithographic presses. Later, when the letterpress departments of Cox & Wyman Ltd. were truncated, some of the redundant equipment was purchased together with one of the machine minders! By 1975 Richard Chapman had retired, the company was under the ownership of the late Terry Key and was being run by a manager. This was to last until the merger with the Iceni Press in 1995.

On Fakenham's new trading estate the parnership of Frost and Matthews set up as jobbing lithographic printers and, with new owners, the name was changed to Taylor Printing in 1982.

The Fakenham Press

Richard Clay

Throughout the late 1970s things were difficult for all UK printers. There were a number of reasons for this, such as foreign printers' quotes being less than the cost of the paper to British printers. Nevertheless Cox & Wyman Ltd. soldiered on. Since Thomas Tilling Ltd. also owned the Heinemann Group of publishers there was some suggestion that they should perhaps send more work to Fakenham & Reading. But this was not the way in which Tillings worked.

By early 1979 Thomas Tilling Ltd. had had enough, the Fakenham factory was renamed The Fakenham Press and almost immediately sold off in the April of that year to Fakenham's old rivals Richard Clay of Bungay. They set about integrating the work of the two print works but, unfortunately in a lot of ways, the products and the systems of the two were very different. Added to this, trading conditions in the print industry, especially the letterpress side of the business, were poor ,with rising costs (not wages) and continued unfair foreign competition. Things came to a head in the middle of 1980 when it was announced that the letterpress departments were to close altogether with the loss of thirty-two jobs. It was the end of an era.

To be fair, there were job losses at Bungay but it was Fakenham which took the brunt of what is now known as downsizing. By the end of the year the closure was complete and the presses had been scrapped, sold or, as in the case of the Centurette press, donated to Gressenhall Rural Life Museum.

By now Wensum Graphics had also gone and some of the workforce had set up business on their own in premises at The Drift. Trading as Colourplan they were providing The Fakenham Press with many of the litho negatives it required for its presses. A sister company, Colourprint, offered small Offset Litho facilities.

At the turn of 1980/81 The Fakenham Press was once again on short-time working and it was clear that printing jobs at cost to compete with foreign suppliers could not continue. By the end of January 1981 *41* administrative jobs numbering seventeen had been shed and the following month ten semi-skilled bindery workers and sixteen filmsetting tradesmen left to be followed in the May by another thirty bindery staff.

During this rapid run-down of The Fakenham Press it emerged that the Clay Group were actively engaged in opening up a printing plant in Singapore, where a lot of the UK competion was coming from. In spite of the assurances given to the workforce it is now known that Clay's mind was made up and Fakenham as well as other bits of the group were to be sacrificed to finance this.

Redundancies continued with four more bindery workers leaving in November when the company stressed that The Fakenham Press would go on trading into 1982. 'We are not out of the wood yet, but we are fighting back and there are signs that we are making a good job of it' a spokesman told The Eastern Daily Press. Following this another thirty workers lost their jobs.

It was now only a matter of time, the trade unions and management burned the midnight oil, an alternative rescue plan was offered to the workforce but only accepted by less than a handful of them, and work went ahead on forming a consortium of workers, banks and others to take over the works.

One hundred and twenty years of book production came to an end on 8th October 1982 when The Fakenham Press closed its doors except for a handful of people who were there to clear up the loose ends. In spite of some considerable effort the consortium had missed out over a short-fall of £250,000 and the following January all the equipment was auctioned off. Within a few years both the Wharfedale Works and the Eagle Star Building had been demolished and all traces removed with the exception of the Miller, Son & Co. Ltd. monogrammed roof brackets from the old bindery which were reused in Miller's Walk shopping mall although one is in the Museum of Gas and Local History along with the 'Cement Books' from the office balcony.

The Fakenham Local History Society obtained a considerable amount of archive material from The Fakenham Press, much of which was deposited with the Record Office in Norwich.

The Holt Rd. premises of the Lancaster Press vacated when it was merged with the Iceni Press. *(Mark Baldwin)*

Below: The Norfolk Chronicle building in 1992 just before it was demolished. *(A. Gill)*

Seed Merchants, Stark & Son took over part of Miller's printing office in Norwich St.

For many years they ran a competition, open to Apprentice Compositors, for the design of their seed catalogue covers.

The last was held in 1959 when the winner was awarded 10/- (50p).

They tried to save the press. Workers and union officials tried to keep the Fakenham Press open. *(Eastern Daily Press)*

Contractors demolish Wyman's splendid front offices in 1987 to leave a rubble strewn open space. *(A. Gill)*

A Tradition Continues
The Last Decades of the Twentieth Century

Fakenham had a long history of print which it was reluctant to give up. Even before The Fakenham Press made its first redundancies some staff were leaving to do their own thing and this continued after the closure.

A group of ex-employees set up Fakenham Photosetting Ltd. as a typesetting bureau while two print finishing companies, Dickens Print Trade Finishers and The Kayleigh Press, were set up by former bindery workers. Others set up a traditional jobbing print works known as Norton & Moyes and two small Offset Litho printers, Norwood Printing and The Iceni Press began trading, the latter company eventually merging with the Lancaster Press in 1995 to form The Lanceni Press. Both Colourplan and Colourprint expanded their workforce by taking on ex-Fakenham Press employees. Individuals also branched out on their own, offering letterpress printing, offset litho printing, graphic design, print management, traditional bookbinding and publishing. Carton printers Key Packaging Ltd. moved into the town to broaden the printing base further.

With so much printing in the town it was little wonder that Fakenham Grammar School operated a press as a society activity during the 1960s and 70s. When the school merged with the Lancastrian School the printing operation became known as The Kobbold Press, eventually aquiring some ex-Cox & Wyman composing equipment.

Books are still produced in Fakenham and are sent all over the world. Every stage of production from the writing to the publishing can still be handled by local companies and many books carry the legend A Product of Fakenham to reinforce this.

Many of these businesses saw their way into the new millennium and the second century of print in Fakenham, a tradition that the town is justly proud of.

What would Chadley Stewardson have thought of it all?